Kyphi
Magic and Art
Creating the Breath of the Gods

Kyphi

Magic and Art

Creating the Breath of the Gods

A Kyphi Making Handbook

By Justine M Crane

ISBN-13: 978-1500494292

ISBN-10: 1500494291

Designed and typeset by Justine M Crane

Manufactured in the U.S.A.

To Shannon, because right now, in this space, in this place in my heart, she is here with me. Thank you sister-mother-mentor-friend.

PREFACE

Becoming a Kyphi maker was a long time coming. I've been blending incense since the 70's, the first experiments being strange combinations of saps and resins, dried elderberries, blackberries, and evergreen fronds found wild-harvesting in the Sierra Nevada Mountains of California. Then I moved onto more sophisticated incense making processes using pine wood shavings, herbs, and spices with a few powdered resins thrown in here and there. Those experiments segued into makko based incense, making dough of herbs, and resins, and essential oils and forming them into little pyramids of scent. Then came the dipping of pre-fabricated bamboo punks into oils and drying them – that was kind of fun. But there was nothing special about making incense like this (except for the wild-harvesting in the Sierra Nevadas). Everything came ready to mix, it was all powdered and prepared, and kind of paint-by-numbers, and you could make dozens of batches in a day. Then I got my hands on a copy of *Kyphi: The Sacred Scent* by Karl Vermillion. I was enamored by the process of Kyphi making, the spiritual aspects, the chanting, the prayers, the reverence for each and every material, the time dedicated to the process – this was definitely not paint-by-numbers incense making. I didn't understand a lot of what Mr. Vermillion wrote   his book is filled with ancient Egyptian hieroglyphics, and is a translation into English from German from Ancient Egyptian. It was confusing. After further research, I came to the conclusion that Kyphi is less about a specific recipe and more about a process of creating magically infused incense using some common core ingredients. So that's what this booklet is about – experimenting upon imagined diverse recipes, and really falling in love with the process and the outcome that is Kyphi. Welcome.

Contents

CHAPTER 1

What is Kyphi?

The word 'Kyphi' is a Greek translation of the Egyptian word 'Kapet' (the Egyptian hieroglyphs spell it 'kp.t' and the pronunciation is a mystery, but the meaning translates to 'grains', a direct reference to incense, and 'pool' or 'mirror', reflecting? Possibly referencing the gods reflecting upon their followers, or the followers reflecting upon their gods?) The Ebers Papyrus was the earliest recipe for Kyphi ever found and it outlined a recipe for Kyphi that was meant to be used as a perfume for clothing (through smoke fumigation), and as a breath 'mint'. The Harris I Papyrus outlined a recipe for Kyphi designed during the Ptolemaic Period of Ancient Egypt which includes notations of gifts given to Pharaoh Ramesses III a few of the ingredients used in the making of Kyphi, which included cinnamon, mastic, pine resin, mint, camel grass (a type of lemongrass?), and sweet flag (calamus). Plutarch, the Greek historian, studied the writings of Manetho, a priest of the Temple of Heliopolis, wherein he discovered a recipe for Kyphi. Here it is revealed that the ingredients used in Kyphi are not ground and added all at once, but instead are each prepared and added on a specific day, in a specific order, with prayers being read throughout the process. Plutarch also states that Kyphi was used as a medicinal, soaked in wine and drunk to induce vivid dreams. Manetho's temple texts have long crumbled away, however the writings and references of this text were immortalized by historians from the 4th century BC through the 8th century AD.

Inscribed on the walls of the Temples Edfu and Philae are found recipes for Kyphi, which, fortunately for us, includes synonyms for the names of some of the ingredients, as well as directions for use. The two recipes from these temples include the same ingredients but differ in the *amounts* of each ingredient. It is here, on these temple walls, that the true complexity of Kyphi is discovered. Not only are the recipes more intricate than what was written by the historians, they include a more complicated manner of preparation, as well as a longer list of ingredients.

Kyphi is prepared using a combination of herbs and raisins soaked in wine and warmed or boiled. Then honey and ground frankincense are combined and boiled. After a period of time, the wine/herbs and the honey/frankincense are combined and then embellished with more resins (usually myrrh). The mixture is then kneaded and dried for a period of 30 to 60 days (because that's how long it takes), then it is rolled or broken into pieces and stored for another few days (or weeks/months) to complete the process. All through the making of Kyphi, prayers are read from special texts and songs are sung to honor the gods for which each ingredient represents.

If we can imagine this scene in our minds ~ the temple workshop's walls lined with baskets overflowing with tears of frankincense and myrrh, heaps of pine resin, bags of pungent juniper berries, camphor and cinnamon bark, bone white orris roots, clay casks of blood red wine, bowls of tiny dried purple raisins, long wooden trenchers filled with honeycomb, and copper vats over open flames brimming with boiling honey and resins. And there, priests and their assistants fill the room with their chanting's hum, and pound the fragrant materials in clay mortars and pour the powders into huge copper bowls as the torchlight cast dancing shadows of the ever-present gods upon the walls. It must have been breathtaking.

In the 7th Century a Greek physician, Paul of Aegina, recorded two different types of Kyphi in his vast medical and historical works ~ a lunar and a solar. According to his writings, the lunar Kyphi consisted of twenty-eight ingredients, while the solar was made of thirty-six ingredients. Elsewhere is found a recipe that includes 50 different materials. This shows a great deal of diversity and flexibility with the ingredients. Then again, creating Kyphi isn't only about the ingredients. The process is equally, if not more, important.

In Ancient Egypt, Kyphi was used ritualistically as the final incense offering of the day. According to information found at the Temple of Heliopolis, the ancient City of the Sun, center of Egyptian culture and religion some 4000 years ago (now modern Cairo), Ancient Egyptians ritualistically burned frankincense at dawn, myrrh at the noon hour, and Kyphi at dusk. The Pyramid Texts, the oldest religious text in the world with over 700 spells and incantations, outlines the exact steps a dead Pharaoh was to take in the afterlife, including the keeping of precious Kyphi.

In addition to being the most regarded incense offering of the day, Kyphi was also a noted medicinal. According to the *De Materia Medica* written by Dioscorides, Kyphi was an important medicine eaten, applied to the skin, burned on a censor, or all of the above. Kyphi was used as a psychological balm, helping to relax and calm those suffering from insomnia and mental illness. Burning Kyphi was also known to precipitate intense and prophetic dreams and to improve meditation – it was considered a magical panacea.

Kyphi is sticky incense. It can be molded and formed into spheres, squares, cones, flat triangles – pretty much any shape desired, then dried and stored in an airtight container until it reaches its prime, which is technically whenever the Kyphi-maker decides it's ready (but no sooner than 30 days after all ingredients are combined). Properly made Kyphi desires songs and prayers during its creation and incubation. Certainly a 'nice' Kyphi can be made without reverence, but a truly spectacular Kyphi is born with all the pomp and circumstance a Kyphi-maker can muster.

Another type of Kyphi exists which includes fewer ingredients and is much simpler to prepare. It is also considered more medicinal than any other type of Kyphi. This type of Kyphi is called 'Kupar', perhaps a version of the word *Kyphi*. Around 200 AD an unidentified scholar began writing a medicinal in Aramaic (Syriac). This scholar's Syriac-Kupar included the traditional honey, wine, and raisins, but differed from the norm by using fewer herbs and reducing the number of resins used.

Rufus of Ephesus (50 AD) wrote down a recipe for Kyphi which included raisins, wine, honey, burnt resin (which type?), and bdellium, a resin like myrrh, and a number of herbs. The preparation was different from the traditional Kyphi as the raisins and honey were combined together, the resins were ground and combined with wine until syrupy, then these two were mixed together, and then the ground herbs were added last. This was then dried and shaped and stored until used.

Again, this proves that like most 'recipes', the individual creator alters the basic ingredients to suit tastes and availability of raw materials.

CHAPTER 2

Basic Kyphi

Kyphi Egyptian-Style

This recipe is roughly ten times smaller than what the Ancient Egyptians would have made at one time, and is not represented as one-hundred percent historically accurate.

7 grams benzoin resin

10 grams calamus root

10 grams mastic

10 grams sandalwood chips

10 grams tragacanth

10 grams cinnamon

10 grams cassia

10 grams camel grass (lemongrass)

14 grams camphor wood (or 7 gr crystals)

20 grams labdanum resin

27 grams galbanum resin

27 grams orris root

27 grams cedar wood (Lebanese?)

54 grams juniper berries

91 grams pine resin

121 grams dried fruit (raisins, dark muscat/burgundy)

121 grams frankincense

151 milliliters fruit juice/fruit wine

115 grams myrrh resin

303 grams honey

1-2 cup dark red grape wine (250 to 500 milliliters)

Begin by grinding by hand in a mortar and pestle (recommended) or with a dedicated coffee grinder the following ingredients (one at a time):

7 gr benzoin resin
10 gr calamus root
10 gr mastic
10 gr sandalwood chips
10 gr tragacanth
10 gr cinnamon
10 gr cassia
10 gr camel grass
14 gr camphor wood or (7 gr camphor crystals)

27 gr orris root
27 gr cedar wood
54 gr juniper berries

Give each item on the list one day to prepare (grind). This list of ingredients will take 12 days to process. As each item is prepared, pour the resultant powder into one large bowl (copper is preferred), eventually combining all the powdered raw materials. Burn resins in a censor, light a beeswax candle, put on meditation music, or create a song or prayer to repeat as each raw material is being prepared. Continue the reverence until the end of the process each day when the bowl is covered and awaits the next raw material's inclusion.

Substitutions: *It is advised to substitute any of the ingredients with a similar ingredient if the original is not easily acquired. This rule of substitution may also be responsible for the many varying historic Kyphi recipes as it is certain that deliveries of raw materials were delayed or voided altogether in ancient times due to robberies or natural disasters or for political reasons. It is feasible that the supplier bringing the goods to the temples could have been killed during his journey, or the goods may have ended up going to Kush instead of Egypt. These unfortunate incidences may have led the temple priests to scramble for suitable substitutions. Substitutions are acceptable.*

Grind all the materials as finely as possible. This helps to spread the ingredients throughout the finished Kyphi. Avoid including large chunks of raw materials by either removing them from the grind, or attempting to grind them further using a dedicated coffee grinder. Orris root, sandalwood chips, camel grass, cinnamon, and cassia can prove troublesome to grind in a mortar and pestle, but attempt to do so anyway.
Once all of the 12 ingredients are ground and combined in a large bowl add between one and two cups (250-500 mls) of the dark red grape wine

to the powdered resins, cover with a clean cloth and set aside for five days.

****

On the first day of the five days of herbs' steeping, light candles and/or burn raw resins on a censor, and continue the ritual prayers and singing, while grinding:

54 gr juniper berry

Add the powdered juniper berry to the steeping herbs and mix well.

****

On the second day of the five days of herbs' steeping, light candles and/or burn raw resins on a censor, and continue the ritual prayers and singing, and prepare:

27 gr galbanum resin

Add the macerated galbanum to the steeping herbs and mix well.

****

On the third day of the five days of herbs' steeping, light candles and/or burn raw resins on a censor, and continue the ritual prayers and singing, and grind:

27 gr orris root

Add the powdered orris root to the steeping herbs and mix well.

****

Add more wine if the incense paste becomes too dry. The point of adding wine is to help draw the fragrant oils from the heart of the resins and spices' powdery depths and bring them to the surface.

On the fourth day of the five days of herbs' steeping, light candles and/or burn raw resins on a censor, and continue the ritual prayers and singing, and grind:

91 gr pine resin

Set aside.

****

On the fifth day of the five days of herbs' steeping, light candles and/or burn raw resins on a censor, and continue the ritual prayers and singing, and grind:

121 gr frankincense tears

Set aside.

****

On the day after the five days of herbs' steeping, light candles and/or burn raw resins on a censor, and continue the ritual prayers and singing, and grind

151 gr myrrh resin

Set aside.

****

On the day after the five days of herbs' steeping (Day 18 in total), sing the ritual prayers and mix together in a glass or metal bowl:

121 grams of raisins, traditionally muscat or burgundy variety

151 grams of fruit juice or fruit wine

It is thought that the Egyptians used palm wine; however procuring palm wine may be difficult. Some recipes for Kyphi contain fruit juices as the soaking menstruum for the raisins, so it isn't a huge diversion from the traditional to use fruit juice rather than palm or fruit wine. Soak the raisins in the juice until the raisins are plump and have taken up a good deal of the fluid. This may take up to 24 hours. It is advisable to place the bowl containing the raisins and fruit juice in the refrigerator as there is a chance of mold growing in warmer temperatures. If the raisin/juice mixture shows signs of mold growth, throw out the batch and begin a new one.

After the raisins have reconstituted, drain out all of the liquid and discard, and then squeeze out the juice from the raisins. Mash the raisins until they are a sticky puree, cover and set aside.

In a Bain Marie, or metal or glass bowl over boiling water, mix together:

121 grams of powdered frankincense

91 grams powdered pine resin

303 grams of honey.

Cook the honey and resins for at least an hour to two hours, or until the resins have melted and the honey has reduced somewhat. This step is important as this is what holds all the other parts of the Kyphi together.

Once the honey/resin mixture has cooled enough to touch without being burned, blend it together with the pureed fruit. It is best to knead the mixture with gloved hands.

Drain the wine from the resins and herbs mixture, then mix the honey/resin/fruit with the resins/herbs/wine mixture and mash together until very well blended. Lastly, add:

115 grams of powdered myrrh resin

Mix well and set the incense aside for a couple of days until it dries just a bit.

After a few days of resting the Kyphi dough, roll the incense dough into cones or balls and set them out to dry. Once the incense is dry enough and isn't tacky, place the pieces into a copper bowl, crock, stoneware or glass jar and set in a cool dark place for a month or more to age and ferment. Rolling the pieces in powdered herbs and resins may help with the drying time, and also add a more intensely fragrant profile to the Kyphi.

CHAPTER 3

Imagined Diversities

This is where the fun of Kyphi making comes into play. Yes, Kyphi making is a spiritual and reverential exercise, but there is no reason it can't be a joyful and creative and fanciful endeavor as well.

There are many ways to tweak and twist the basic Egyptian style Kyphi recipe to suit specific needs. If a meditation Kyphi is needed, adding to or substituting with herbs and resins which provide a meditative aura will help bring the meditation Kyphi to fruition. For example, replacing all the resins in the basic recipe with frankincense and myrrh, throwing in dried and powdered rose petals as a substitute for calamus and juniper, and increasing the amount of orris root powder may help define the meditation Kyphi. The 'trick', if there is a trick, is to keep the resins at about twice the amount as the herbs, and both well over the amount of raisins – i.e. four parts resins to two parts herbs. Honey should be around three parts of the total, and the raisins, or other dried fruit, at about one part. This ensures a balance of fragrant materials to base materials (raisins/honey).

The raisins and honey serve as binders and provide a good deal of the smoke involved in burning the incense, while the resins and herbs provide the aromatic portion of the Kyphi (and, obviously, smoke upon burning).

Additions of essential oils, absolutes, and plant-based concretes to Kyphi are also acceptable, especially if the essential oil or other natural plant-based aromatic extraction is being used as a substitute for a resin or herb that is difficult to locate. Adding essential oils or other fluid aromatics may extend the drying period of the finished Kyphi. For example, replacing seven grams of camphor wood in the basic Kyphi recipe with camphor crystals is fine, as is replacing the seven grams of camphor wood with five or six drops of pure camphor essential oil. Also adding a few drops of other essential oils may compliment the Kyphi -- for example, to boost the myrrh scent, or the frankincense scent, or add a twist of rose, add in a few drops of the essential oils of these elements. This would be the last step before ageing and drying the incense.

Soaking the raisins (or dried fruit) in hard liquor (gin or rum or whiskey), or soaking them in hydrosol is also acceptable, and adds a layer of scent complexity to the finished Kyphi.

Kyphi Recipe

Golden Kyphi

50 g sun dried non-sulfated apricots

50 g golden raisins

200 g naturally rose flavored wine or rose hydrosol

      In a bowl combine the apricots, raisins, and wine or hydrosol, cover and refrigerate.

34 g Sumatran benzoin

28 g myrrh

Grind the benzoin and myrrh separately, combine in a large bowl, and set aside for one day.

28 g Egyptian chamomile

Grind the chamomile, combine with the benzoin/myrrh mixture and set aside for one day.

5 g aloes wood

Grind the aloes wood and combine with the other dried herbs/resins, and set aside for one day.

4 g orris root

28 g galangal

30 g green cardamom pods

30 g calamus root

50 g pink rose petals

50 g sandalwood chips

Grind each ingredient separately, and combine with the other dried herbs/resins in the bowl, then set the bowl aside for one day.

10 g thyme

Grind the thyme and combine it with the other dried herbs/resins in the bowl.

1-2 cups white wine

Pour the white wine into the bowl containing the herbs and resin powders. Mix well, kneading with gloved hands. Add more wine if the mixture is too dry. The consistency of the mixture should resemble a slightly loose paste. Cover the bowl and set aside for five days.

At the end of the five days, remove the raisins/apricots and wine from the refrigerator and pour off all the liquid, squeezing out any excess from the fruit. Mash the fruit until it forms a thick paste.

Take the herbs/resins bowl and pour off the white wine, squeeze any excess fluid out and discard. Mix the fruit/wine mixture into the herbs/resins mixture and knead until cohesive.

300 g honey (neem works best for this recipe)

300 g frankincense

Grind the frankincense and add to a Bain Marie with the honey. Boil the mixture on medium/low heat for one or two hours, until the resin is nearly melted. Stir frequently and check for scorching. Remove from the heat and allow the mixture to cool so that it can be handled. Once cool, slowly pour the honey/frankincense syrup into the fruit/resin/herbs mixture and blend well, using gloved hands. Leave the mixture in the bowl to dry for a few days, kneading often to aerate the mixture. Once the mixture is tacky and holds together, add five drops each of the following essential oils:

Frankincense

Myrrh

Styrax

Labdanum

Cedar wood

Coriander

Galbanum

Spikenard

      Mix the essential oils into the Kyphi paste, kneading with gloved hands. Allow the Kyphi paste to dry until tacky, and then begin shaping into balls or cones and dry the bits on waxed or parchment paper. Dry the incense for as long as it takes to prevent the pieces from sticking together, and then put all the pieces in a copper bowl, crock, or large bowl, and cover. Set aside for 30-60 days before using.

Syriac-Kupar Recipe

Syriac-Kupar is an extremely simple type of incense to make in comparison to Kyphi. This recipe uses fewer herbs, no fruit, and turns out a much smaller batch of incense at the end than what are gained making Kyphi. Reverence and patience are still applied to the making of Syriac-Kupar.

2 g orris root

2 g jasmine sambac concrete

6 g oak moss (the actual moss)

14 g pine resin

14 g sandalwood chips

28 g dark red wine

28 g elemi resin

28 g white fir resin

30 g pink rose petals

140 g frankincense resin

115 g myrrh resin

300 g dark honey (black sage works best for this recipe)

Grind oak moss, orris root, and sandalwood chips separately, combine in a large bowl, and pour in the dark red wine, mix well, set aside in the refrigerator for a few days.

When the herbs/wine mixture has set for a few days, grind the pine resin, frankincense resin, and myrrh resin separately and mix together in a Bain Marie with the 300 grams of dark honey. Bring to a boil on medium/low heat and boil for one to two hours, until cohesive.

Remove the herbs/wine mixture from the refrigerator and drain any excess wine from the bowl, if any. Mix the honey/resin into the herbs/wine and mix well, using gloved hands. Knead in the elemi resin, the white fir resin (grind this resin if it is not soft), and the jasmine sambac concrete. Line a rectangular cake pan with parchment paper and pour the Syriac-Kupar onto the paper and set the cake pan out of the way so the incense can dry in the open air. Every day, flip the incense syrup over and knead it to expose the less dry parts, and set it aside to dry another 24 hours. This process will take weeks (six to eight weeks or more). Once the incense becomes tacky and moldable, roll it into spheres, and roll the spheres in powdered pink rose petals. Set aside to dry another few weeks to a month or more.

Bibliography

Ancient Egypt Online (www.ancientegyptonline.co.uk)

De Materia Medica, Dioscorides

Kyphi: The Sacred Scent, Karl Vermillion

The Medical Works of Paulus Aegineta, the Greek Physician: Tr. Into English; with a Copious Commentary Containing a Comprehensive View of the Knowledge Possessed by the Greeks, Romans, and Arabians, on All Subjects Connected with Medicine and Surgery, Paul of Aegina (historian)

Sacred Luxuries: Fragrance, Aromatherapy, and Cosmetics in Ancient Egypt, Lise Manniche

www.ingramcontent.com/pod-product-compliance
Lightning Source LLC
Chambersburg PA
CBHW081417170526
45166CB00010B/3372